'BEHIND DOOR NUMBER NOW'

LEE MARION HOROWITZ
AUTHOR

ELIZABETH ESTHER KELLY
ILLUSTRATOR

BEHIND DOOR NUMBER NOW
IS AN OVERSIZED CAMEL COLORED PLUSH PLEATHER CHAIR WITH A LEOPARD PRINT FOOTSTOOL JUST SITTING THERE BECKONING LILA TO COME AND HAVE A SIT, RELAX AND BE COOL HANG OUT FOR A BIT

What would you like to find in your treasure box?
What are some thought and feeling habits you would like to compost?
Why?
Can you name 3 feelings that you enjoy?
Can you name 3 feelings that are difficult for you?
Can you bring a tender heart and touch to these feelings?

THE END

FOR NOW

www.ingramcontent.com/pod-product-compliance
Lightning Source LLC
Chambersburg PA
CBHW041404010526
44107CB00015B/1066